Other Books by the Authors

The Haiku Blues
Deluxe Limited Edition

The Haiku Blues
Trade Edition

Full Spectrum of Blue

The Constitutional Blues

The Divorce Blues

The Soul-Bendin' Blues

Origionally published in
The Haiku Blues
Haiku that will take you on a journey through pain, love, politics and soul

By Ted becker and Patricia Lantz

WIPF & STOCK · Eugene, Oregon

Wipf and Stock Publishers
199 W 8th Ave, Suite 3
Eugene, OR 97401

Soul Bendin' Blues
By Becker, Ted L. and Lantz, Patricia
Copyright©2015 by Becker, Ted L.
ISBN 13: 978-1-5326-3650-9
Publication date 6/30/2017
Previously published by Blurb, 2015

Table of Contents

The Haiku Blues

I write haiku when
I'm feelin' blue and when love and
pain make me want to.

Welcome to God's Penal Colony

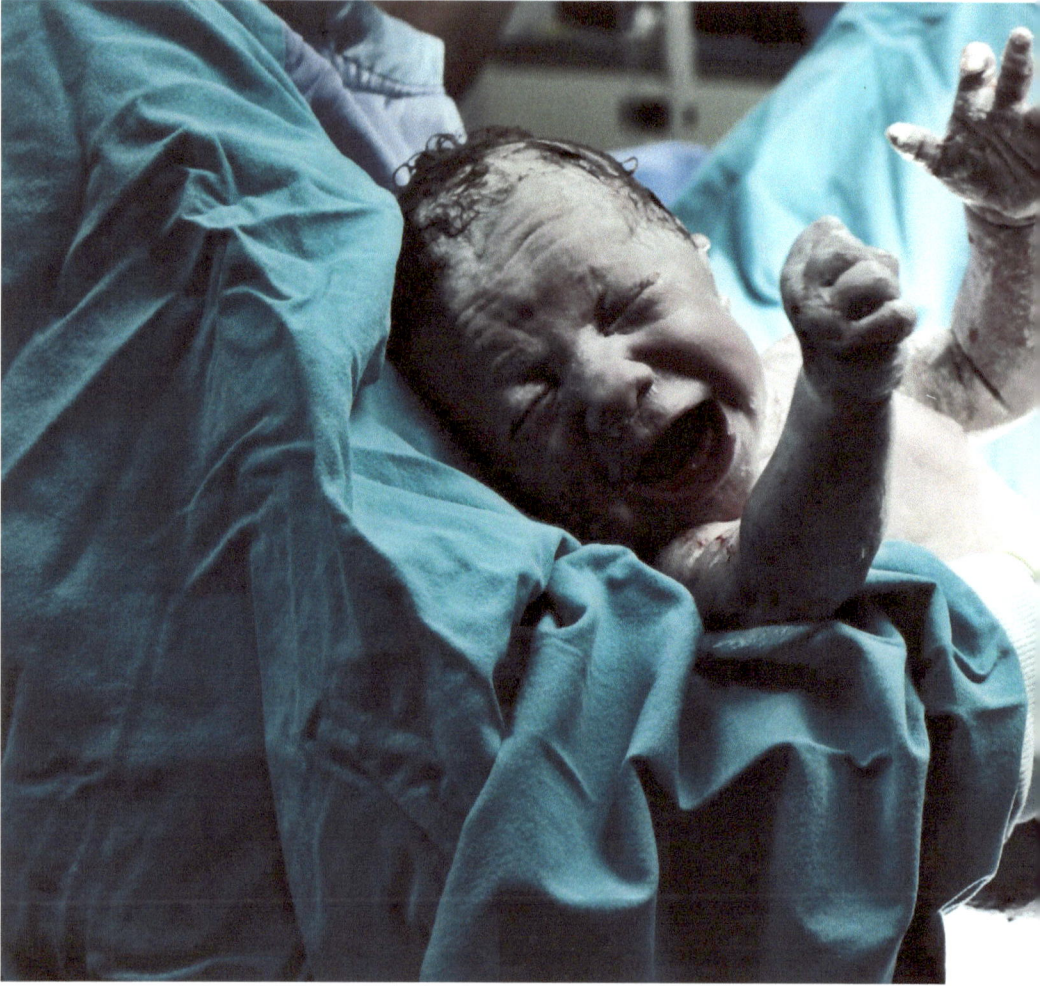

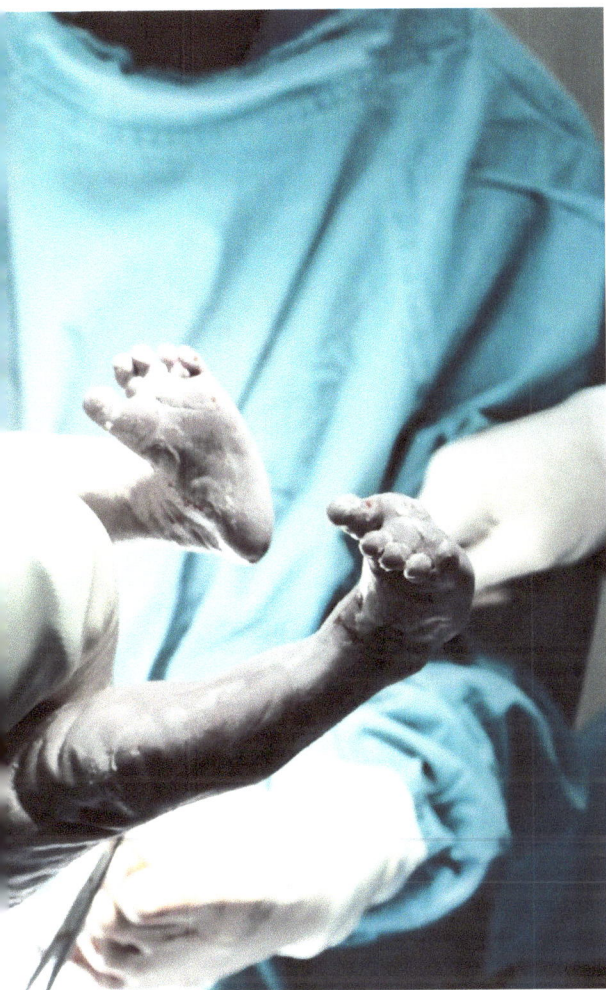

No wonder babes cry
when birthed to this world of hurt.
Their sentence is life.

Down Hill Racer

Over the hill: Then
cane, crutches, wheelchair, gurney,
deathbed, pall. That's y'all.

それを
のよ今み
りうつをえ
いョ以あぐも
うると
あをで
とそで
それを
すれてきる
らひ
ョ

The Divine Idea of Orgasm

The greatest pleasure
in human life are spasms
that procreate it.

Sexual Spirituality

Orgasmic fireworks.
Imploding chasms. Two out
of body bodies.

To My Alter Ego in a Parallel Universe

My mirror image
life's exquisite. When mine on
Earth cracks, I'll visit.

Slippery Joy, Sticky Sorrow

Joy slips away so
quick from you, while sadness sticks
to your heart like glue.

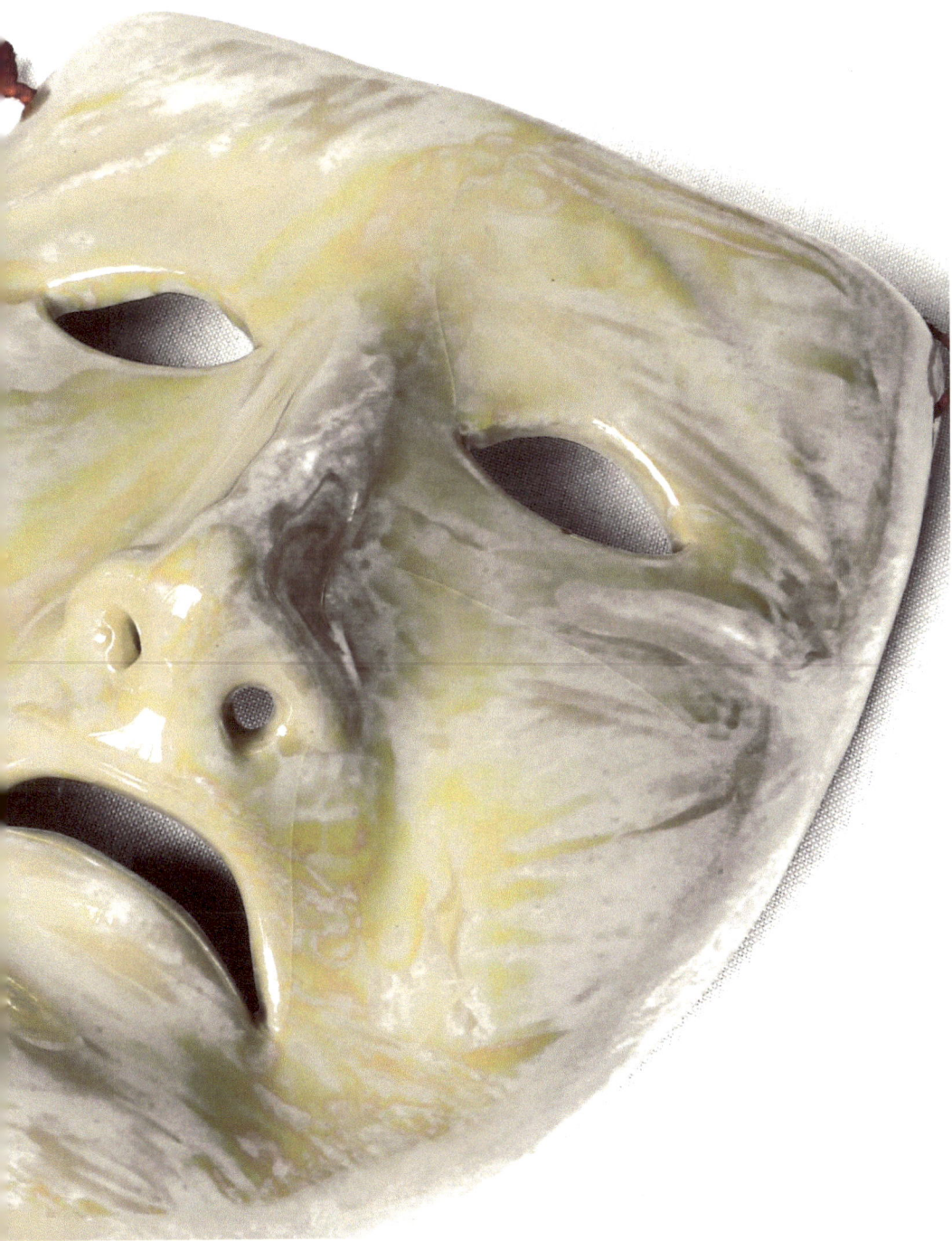

Will You Like What You See?

Your life may flash in
your eyes before you die and
you should want to look.

True Love Off Earth

The only pure love
you'll find off this deviled egg
is in God's presence.

Seeing the Light

Sparkling ripples in
a light stream into me through
a seam in the air.

Baptized at 72

I chose baptism
in my dotage, not as faith,
but for my homage.

Heavenly Missions

Not coincidence.
A chance to play God's angel,
granted by request.

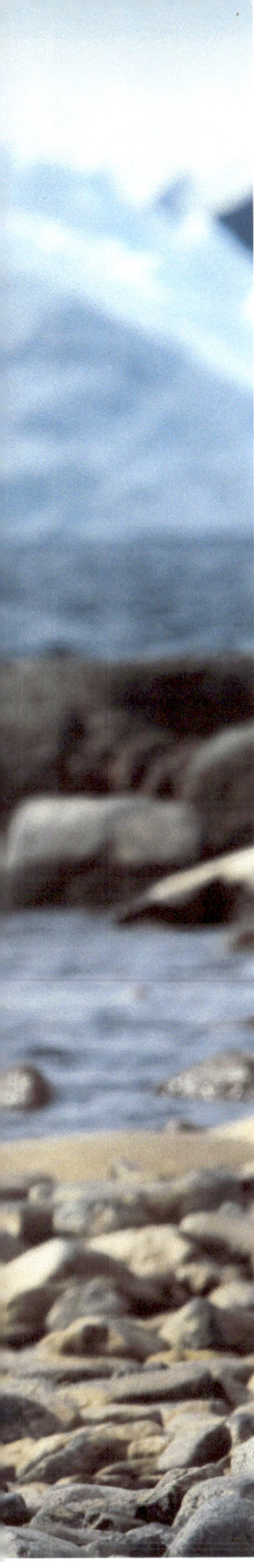

How to Avoid a Deadly Sin

Be not proud of what's
achieved, just grateful for its
intended purpose.

Only God Hears

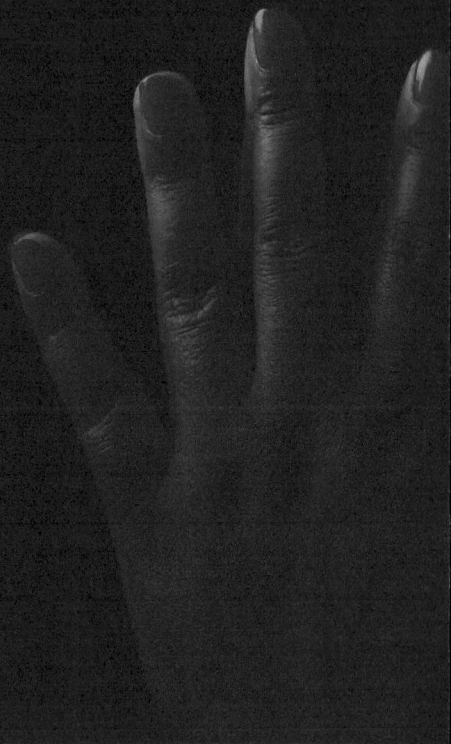

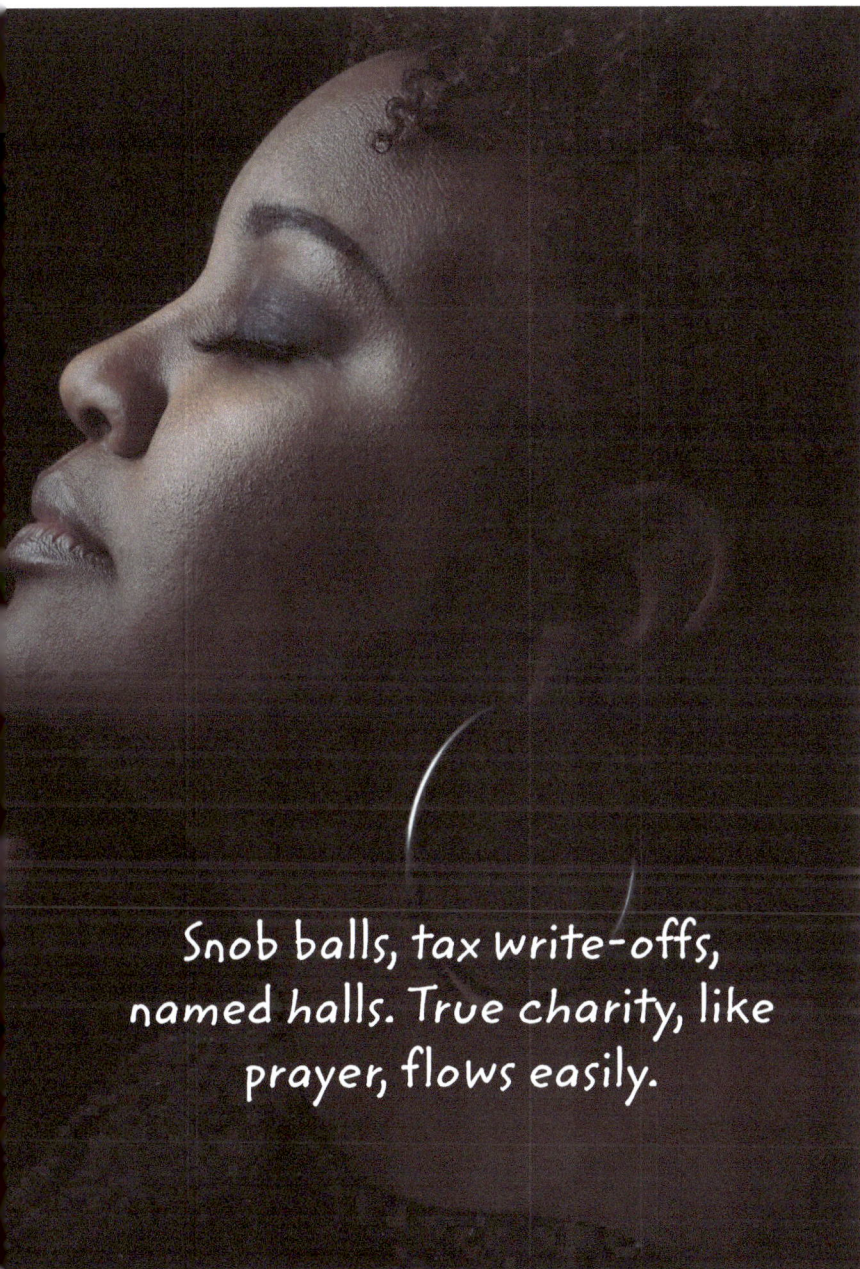

Snob balls, tax write-offs, named halls. True charity, like prayer, flows easily.

When God Smiles and Sighs

When we poke fun at
ourselves, God smiles. When we mock
others, She just sighs.

Lucky in Life

Life self-realized
and with no regrets, is as
lucky as it gets.

In the Wake of Rapture

Best yield from here with
sorrow, not blame. Please save me
from this place again.

Surfing Infinity

Wave after wave of
shiny froth roaring: Welcome!
Ride us to Heaven.

Flying Out

Some die with loved ones
grieving by, others leave with
God alone, to fly.

Good Way to Go

When death is near, if
you can leave ecstatic, you'll
avoid all traffic.

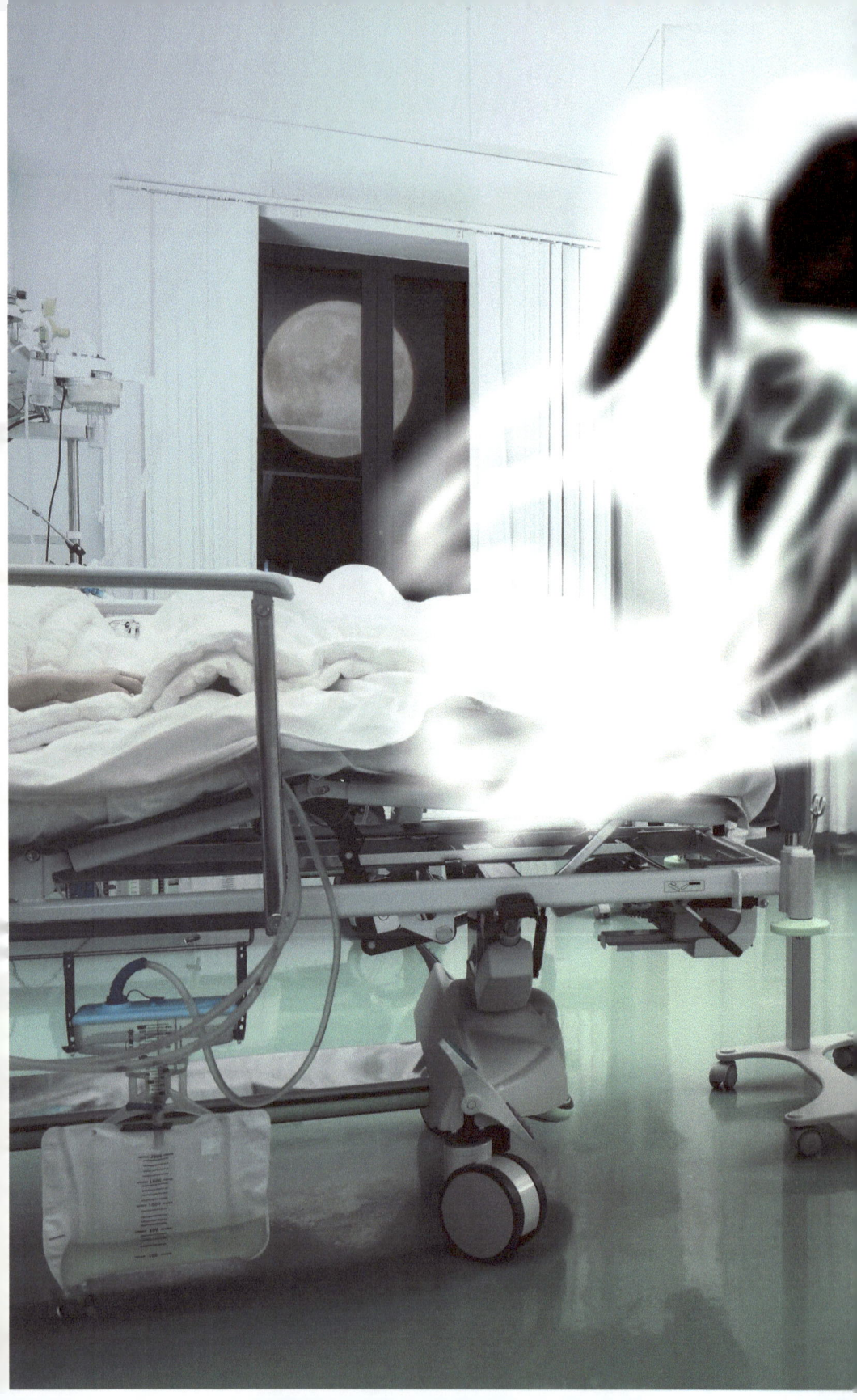

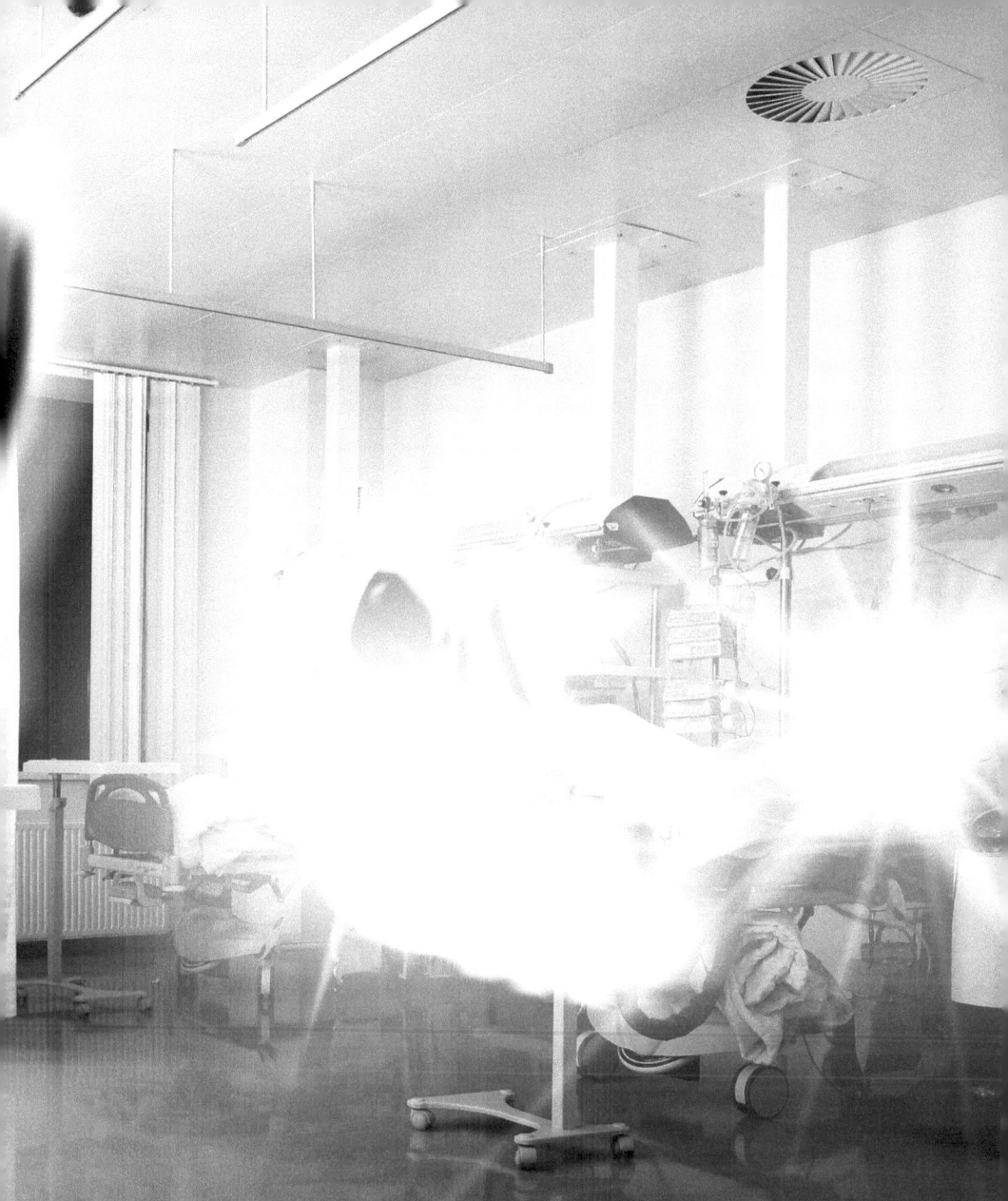

Brighter is Lighter

The brighter is your
incandescence, the lighter
is your transcendence.

Blood Twilights

Translucent glow, low
in blood sky. Awesome, apt end
to a day or life.

Alone on the Bridge of Gratitude
(A Zen Poem of Many Haikus)

I.

I've lived well and long
without waiting for cell phone
songs to deflect me.

II.

Appreciate death:
luxuriate in each step,
savor precious breaths.

III.

Lately, I find much
fewer eyes to meet, with these
cell phones, now replete.

IV.

Catch those vacant glares,
staring nowhere, listening:
neither here nor there.

V.

Bees are bizzy, on
the go, always buzzing to
and fro. Not alone!

VI.

You may see one... but
there are connections, unseen,
with strong directions.

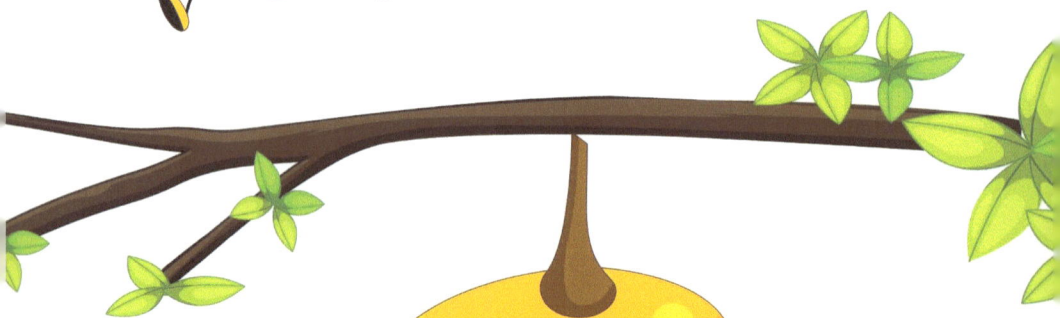

VII.

They are the workers,
makers of money, for their
hives... banks of honey.

VIII.

No drone knows where it's been. Electric pulleys draw it back to the Queen.

IX.

'Star Trek' got it right:
'Borgs' and humans locked in flight:
The outcome? In doubt.

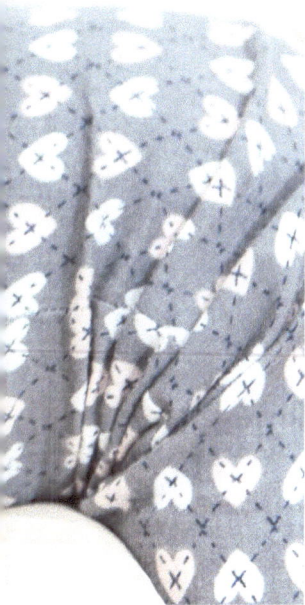

X.

Electronic swarms
with material goals, lone
critters soothing souls.

XI.

One needs leeway, time
on hold, family at bay,
brain on feline play.

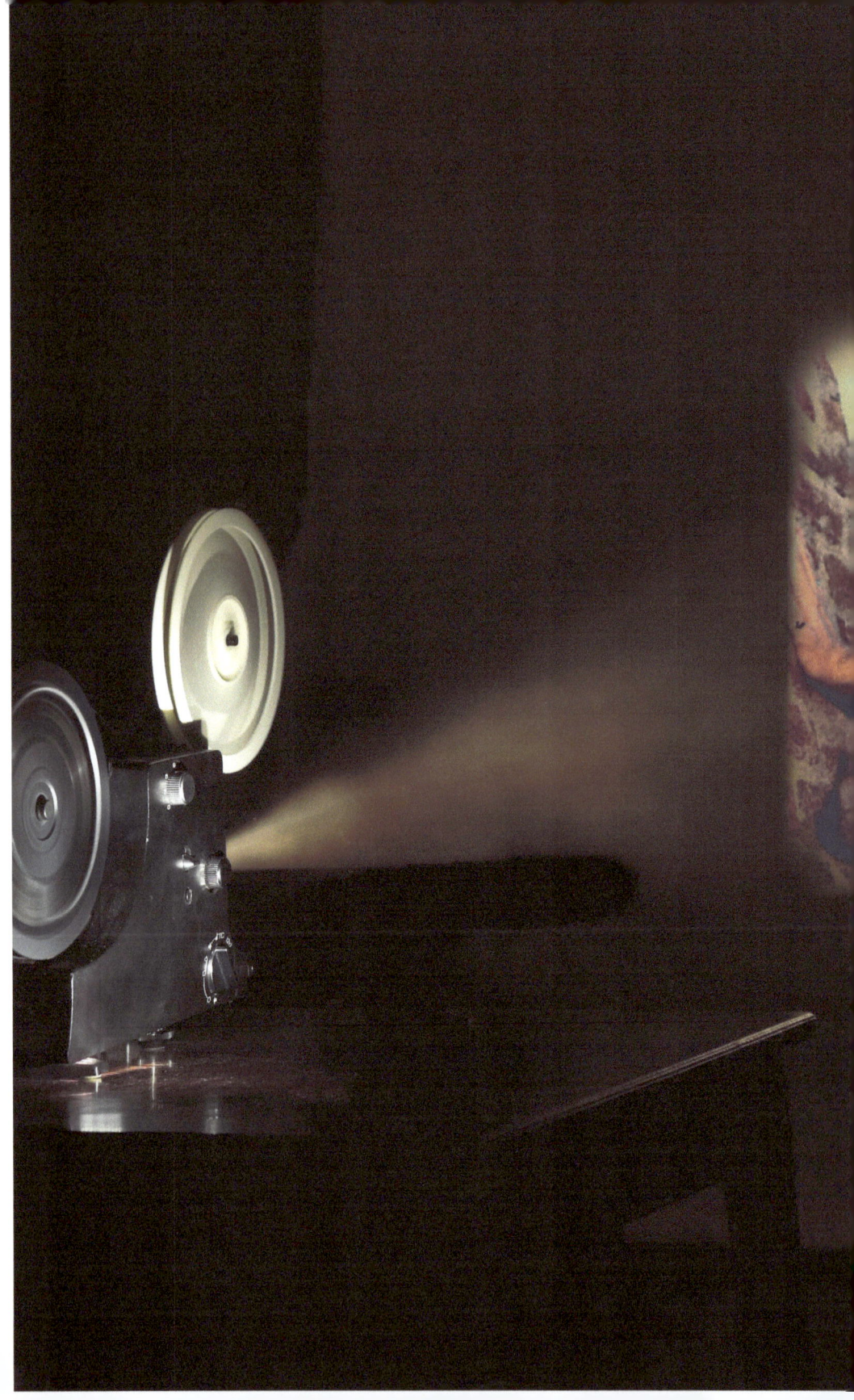

Finale
(in 7 Zenned Haikus)

So, has my life been
filmed illusions projected
on the cells inside

my lame brain by a
Deus ex Machina? Or
was it as a frame

through a light flashing
so quickly and unnoticed
by an audience

of all those who paid
the price to sit in judgment?
Oh, it was real. Yeah!

Every second,
every smell, every
taste, every sight.

Every choice. Each
loss was a gift from the best
producer, the best

screenwriter: the best
director any soul could have
to play their best role.

About the Authors

Ted Becker has led many lives: Class clown of his high school;. sports editor of his college newspaper; consumer researcher for a large Madison Avenue advertising agency; member of the legal staff for the Attorney General of New Jersey; military intelligence; law school professor; oft-cited academic; mediator; online journal editor; author of 14 books on law, politics and political science.

Patricia Lantz is a former stylist and business owner, an Atlanta based counseling astrologer, writer and editor of astrology on AllThingsHealing.com, an online community dedicated to holistic and alternative healing of mind, body, spirit and planet.

Special Offer

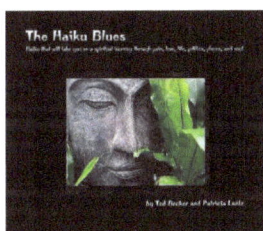

The Haiku Blues, Deluxe Limited Edition is in coffee book format, 13" x 11" and 170 pages, printed on highest quality photo paper. It's amazing to look at and at times seems like it's printed in 3D. This is not a book you will put on a shelf and forget. It's a book that will enhance your décor and that you'll want constantly be within easy reach so you easily pick it up and meditate on some of your favorites. Given its size and dazzling quality, we are offering only 300 of our "Deluxe Limited Edition" at $295. Each book will be numbered and inscribed by the authors in any way you request (that's legal and doesn't violate The Patriot Act). If interested and want more details just email, becker.ted@gmail.com or write Dr. Ted Becker, 4707 Pebble Shore Drive, Opelika, AL 36804, for more details.